Facts About the Badger

By Lisa Strattin

Facts for Kids Picture Books by Lisa Strattin

Little Blue Penguin, Vol 92

Chipmunk, Vol 5

Frilled Lizard, Vol 39

Blue and Gold Macaw, Vol 13

Poison Dart Frogs, Vol 50

Blue Tarantula, Vol 115

African Elephants, Vol 8

Amur Leopard, Vol 89

Sabre Tooth Tiger, Vol 167

Baboon, Vol 174

Sign Up for New Release Emails Here

http://LisaStrattin.com/subscribe-here

Monthly Surprise Box

http://KidCraftsByLisa.com

All information in this book has been carefully researched and checked for factual accuracy. However, the author and publisher makes no warranty, express or implied, that the information contained herein is appropriate for every individual, situation or purpose and assume no responsibility for errors or omissions. The reader assumes the risk and full responsibility for all actions, and the author will not be held responsible for any loss or damage, whether consequential, incidental, special or otherwise, that may result from the information presented in this book.

All images are free for use or purchased from stock photo sites for commercial use.

Some coloring pages might be of the general species due to lack of available images.

I have relied on my own observations as well as many different sources for this book and I have done my best to check facts and give credit where it is due. In the event that any material is used without proper permission, please contact me so that the oversight can be corrected.

COVER IMAGE

By BadgerHero - Own work, CC BY-SA 3.0,
https://commons.wikimedia.org/w/index.php?curid=7428454

ADDITIONAL IMAGES

SPECIAL THANKS TO LARRY LAMSA

https://www.flickr.com/photos/larry1732/6138869804/

https://www.flickr.com/photos/larry1732/9476838446/

https://www.flickr.com/photos/larry1732/9476835808/

https://www.flickr.com/photos/canopic/3614829127/

https://www.flickr.com/photos/larry1732/6138868938/

https://www.flickr.com/photos/blmidaho/28516914841/

https://www.flickr.com/photos/nwcouncil/7177470009/

https://www.flickr.com/photos/santamonicamtns/39995010991/

https://www.flickr.com/photos/larry1732/14763891207/

https://www.flickr.com/photos/larry1732/15104710702/

Contents

INTRODUCTION

The badger is related to otters, polecats, weasels, and ferrets.

The largest is the European badger. The ones just a bit smaller are the American Badger, the Honey Badger and the Hog Badger. The smallest are the Stink Badger and the Ferret Badger.

CHARACTERISTICS

Some Badgers are solitary, moving from place to place, while others live in family-type clans called *cetes*, that can be as few as 2 animals or as many as 15. That is a pretty big family!

They can run as fast as 19 miles per hour, but only for a short period of time. They are nocturnal, this means they mostly sleep during the day and come out to look for food at night.

APPEARANCE

Badgers have wide and short bodies, and short legs which they use for digging. Their heads are long with very small ears. The Stink Badger has a very short tail, while the Ferret Badger has a much longer one. The length of their tail depends on the species of Badger.

Their black face with white markings make them easily identified in the wild. They also have a grey body, dark legs, and a lighter color on their belly. They sometimes have a light colored stripe that runs from nose-to-tail.

REPRODUCTION

Females give birth in the early Springtime, to 1 to 5 young in a litter, but the usual litter size is 3 babies. Females can mate when they are 4 months old but they usually don't until they are a year old. Males are around 2 years old before they look for a partner to mate. They breed once per year.

LIFE SPAN

Badgers live to be from 4 to 10 years of age

SIZE

Adult Badgers can be as short as 16 inches long to almost 30 inches long. They weigh from 24 to 30 pounds, on average. So, this means they are similar to the size of many dogs we keep as pets.

HABITAT

Badgers all live underground in burrows. Sometimes, these burrow homes can be large with different rooms and tunnels leading throughout a significant area.

DIET

Badgers are omnivores. This means they eat plants and meat. They like earthworms, insects, grubs, reptiles, birds, small mammals, frogs, fruit and some roots. They usually live where there are plenty of bugs and vegetation to eat!

ENEMIES

Eagles and Wildcats are known to hunt Badgers. They have long claws to protect themselves, but they are not really strong enough to fight off an Eagle or Wildcat once they are caught.

SUITABILITY AS PETS

Badgers are kept as pets in some areas of the world and are pretty easy to tame. However, it is illegal to keep them in the United Kingdom because they are a protected animal there.

If you want to keep one as a pet, be sure to check your local laws to make sure you won't get in trouble.

However, if you just want to see some Badgers, there might be a habitat at your local zoo where you can watch them up close.

COLOR ME

COLOR ME

COLOR ME

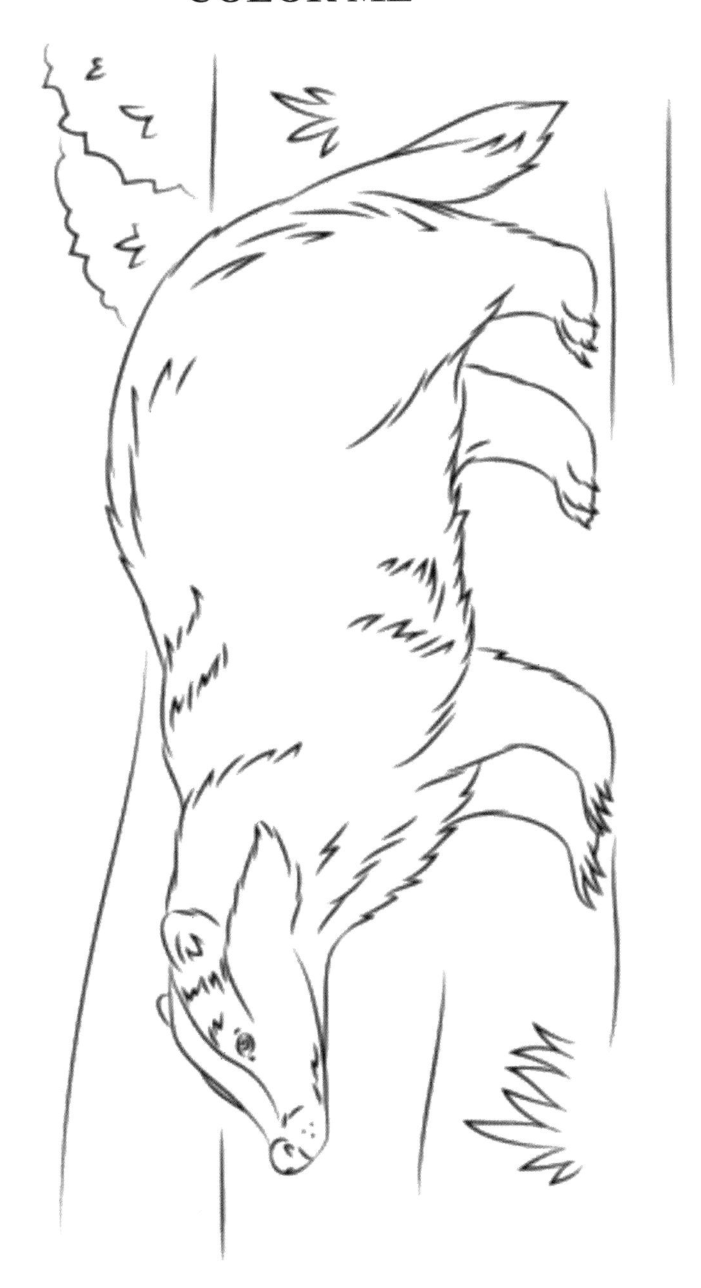

COLOR ME

COLOR ME

COLOR ME

COLOR ME

COLOR ME

COLOR ME

COLOR ME

Please leave me a review here:

http://lisastrattin.com/Review-Vol-306

For more Kindle Downloads Visit Lisa Strattin Author Page on Amazon Author Central

http://amazon.com/author/lisastrattin

To see upcoming titles, visit my website at LisaStrattin.com– all books available on kindle!

http://lisastrattin.com

PLUSH BADGER TOY

You can get one by copying and pasting this link into your browser:

http://lisastrattin.com/PlushBadger

MONTHLY SURPRISE BOX

Get yours by copying and pasting this link into your browser

http://KidCraftsByLisa.com

Printed in Great
Britain
by Amazon